I CAN DRAW and COLOR people

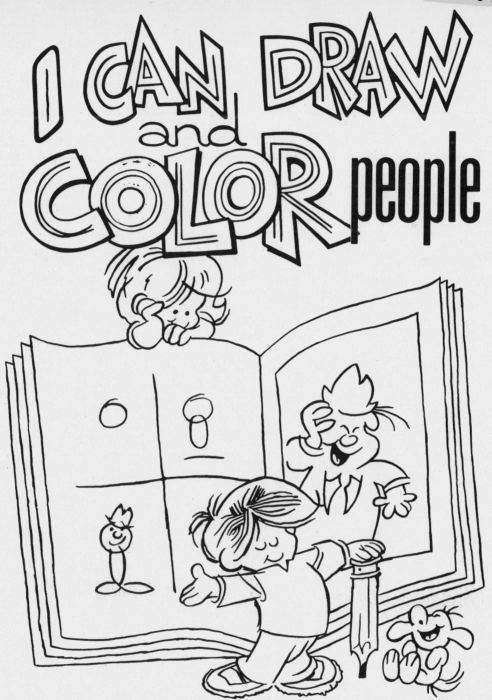

by Thomas Yackutis / Gasper Vaccaro

So you want to learn to draw and color? So did Rembrandt and other famous painters when they were your age. They drew and colored and colored and drew until they became very good at it. So can you. To be good at <u>anything</u>, you have to do it a lot. In this book you'll have fun as you draw and color.

Before you start, you have to decide what you are going to draw and color. Stop and think about it. You have to think about it so hard that you can see what you are going to draw and color in your head . . . then you copy it onto the paper. Easy, right? What's on the paper will never be as good as what you saw in your head, but it will be better than if you just go ahead and start scribbling.

Ask yourself, "How do I feel about what I'm drawing and coloring?" Suppose you want to draw a dog: What kind of a dog will it be?

A mean dog?   A nice dog?   Your dog?

What kind of a dog do you see in your head? Draw <u>that</u> dog.

Is the dog shaped like a triangle, a circle, a square, or a blob?

Will you draw it with straight lines, curvy lines, or wiggly, squiggly lines?

Will your dog (or your person or dinosaur or anything) be red? Blue? Yellow, black, brown? Color can be important. If a sky is blue, for example, it probably means that it is a nice day. If the sky's red, it could mean that there is a big fire, or a volcano erupting, or perhaps a sunset. What do you want your colors to say?

Let's think about shape. Shapes can be circles, squares, rectangles, triangles, or curves. Everything you draw will be a combination of shapes. Throughout this book we'll give you hints on what shapes to use to draw heads, bodies, and other parts. You'll see that many of the lines on the shapes disappear in the next drawing. That's because artists erase those shapes as they draw more and more of the piece of art, to make it look more real. Which looks better,

this   or this?

What's the difference? We got rid of some of the shape lines! You can do that too! Here's another hint: each drawing is divided into four parts. The first three will be easy. Putting the finishing touches on the fourth one will be a little harder. If you want to, you can stop at the third drawing. If you want to add more detail, go on to the fourth. It's up to you! As you look at the first picture, start drawing its lines in the space on the next page. There's plenty of room for your whole drawing. Add as much as you like, then color your drawing and the scene. Don't forget, you're the artist! Okay. Start drawing and coloring. Have fun!

Drawing with Basic Shapes

- Remember: 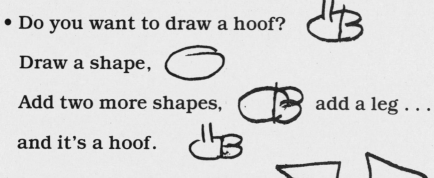 = Shapes!
- Combine these shapes and you can draw anything.
- Do you want to draw a foot?

  Draw a shape 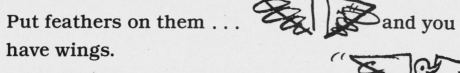 . . .

  Put toes on it . . . and it's a foot.

- Do you want to draw a hoof?

  Draw a shape,

  Add two more shapes, add a leg . . .

  and it's a hoof.

- Wings? Draw two shapes.

  Put feathers on them . . . and you have wings.

  Add some more shapes and it's a duck.

- Claws? Draw some bananas.

  Add nails and a leg 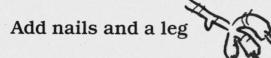 and you get claws.

- Draw shapes, combine them with action and gesture and you're an artist. It's easy and lots of fun.

Putting Excitement Into Your Art

• Remember: Action! Gesture!

• This is a ball .

It bounces so . . . down and up. Right?

It flies through the air .

It hits a bat .

and . . . Got it?

(Not yet? Here's more.)

• A man .

A man leaning .

He leans too far .

He's flat on the ground .

Somehow he got up and now he's walking .

Now he's running .

He skids to a stop . SKID

He falls down .

Got it? It's fun and easy.

People

If there were one hundred and seventy zillion people in the world, no two would be exactly alike. Fat, skinny....Tall, short....Black, white, brown....Long legs, bow legs....Straight hair, curly hair.... There is no limit to the number of ways people are put together, but mostly they have one head, four limbs, only one nose and... well, you know...they look like you. You could draw people with eight limbs and more than one nose but nobody would believe that they are people.

When you draw people, try not to be mean and hurt their feelings. Drawings should be fun, not cruel.

The left-hand page shows you <u>HOW</u> and the right-hand page shows you <u>WHERE</u>. Here's a secret. When we look at a picture of a person the first thing we look at are the eyes. Then we look at the hands, then everything else; so be extra careful with the eyes.

How tall are people?

Some are tall, some not.

Cartoon people are often three heads tall, but you can make them any size you want.

Real people are often five or six heads tall.

How fat are people?

People are all sorts of fat or skinny.

But it does help if all their heads are about the same size.

How funny are people?

They are as funny as you can imagine.

How they look is important. What they do is important.

What you mean them to be is the most important.

Here we see a reasonable person reasoning with a silly person.

Let's start out with your average man. He's standing straight.

He has a round head and two oval feet. What details make him different from anybody else?

He has a round nose and round ears. A few lines for his body and hat are a good idea.

There he is, different from anybody else. He's one of a kind.

Draw him lined up with his buddies ready to go to work. See?
No two are quite alike.

Let's do a man running. Start with a circle and two curved lines.

He's running hard. Add hair, curved lines for arms, and legs.

He's running real hard. You can stop here or go on.

I wonder what he's running from? Puffs of dust show how fast he's going.

Oh! Wow! Yikes!

Let's do a woman running. She's a circle and some curved lines for body, legs, and feet.

She's running hard. Add puffy hair, arms, and shoes.

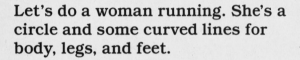

She's running real hard. Now it's time for some round eyes and some nice clothes.

I wonder what she's running from? Draw her fur piece, hat, and clouds of dust to show she's going fast!

She should not wear that fur piece on the first day
of fox-hunting season.

Here's a circle and three curved lines.

Always start with the action . . . and the shapes. He needs a half-oval hat and some V's for his coat. Start his boots and hands, too.

You can put a hose in his hands.

He's ready to put out a fire.

There's no barbecue today.

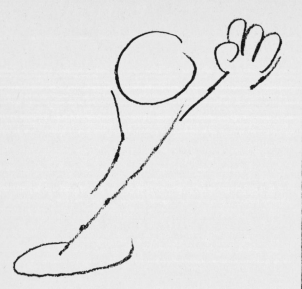

It's worth repeating because it's important: Always start with the gesture or action. Draw a round head, a hand, and three curved lines.

Then the shapes . . . circles for feet, simple clothes, and a hat.

Then the details, and you have it.

Don't forget his badge. He's Gasparo the policeman.

Everybody has to wait for his friends to cross the street.

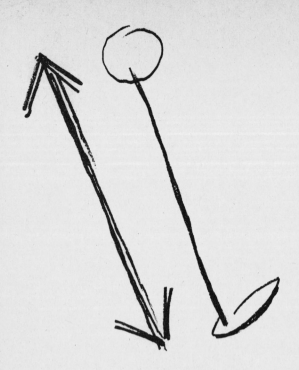

This guy is marching. See how off balance he is? He's a slanted line, a sharp oval, and a round head.

But his other leg catches up with him.

He's a soldier. Give him a rifle and a helmet. His arm is at his side. You can stop here or go on.

He's a sergeant.

Remember how we said everybody was different?
Well, not always. Not in Sergeant Farrell's company.

Start with a squiggly line and a circle. Let's do something unusual. Always put down your lines and shapes first.

Add a nose and straight lines for arms. He needs hands, too.

What is this we are drawing? Fill out the body with another curved line.

His name is Ralph and he is a good acrobat.

If you don't believe that Ralph is a good acrobat, ask the parakeets. They'll tell you.

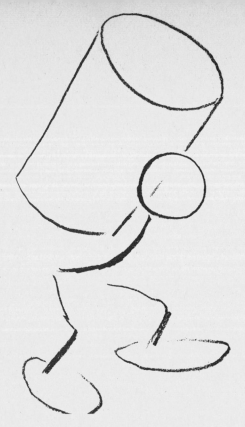

Let's draw something heavy. Start with a cylinder, a circle, some curved lines, and oval shoes.

What is he carrying? Add hands, clothes, and a line for a hat.

Finish his face, hat, overalls, and shoes. You can stop now or go on.

He's a trash collector.

Being a trash collector is hard work. But you make a lot of friends.

Let's do a king. You need lots of curved lines. Make a crown, round face, and cape.

Being a king is not all that easy. Give him a scepter and a long nose.

Not everybody can be a king.

It's a hard job but somebody has to do it.

But there are some good things about being a king.

What is this little girl doing? Start her with a round head and a few curved lines for her body, feet, and arms.

She's stomping on something. She looks angry. Give her fluffy hair and a frown. What, I wonder, is she stomping on?

Curved lines will show that her foot is moving.

They are ants! The kind that bite.

The ants might ruin the family picnic.

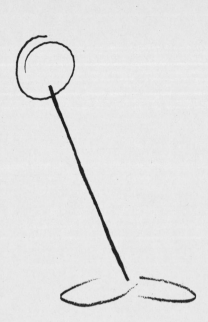

Let's do another off-balance picture. Start with a slanted line, two ovals, and a circle.

His hat looks like a tulip. His body is almost pear-shaped. Add a moustache.

He's a long, tall Texan. Give him boots, a tie, and a jacket. You can stop here if you wish.

Is he the last long, tall Texan in the West?

Nope! There are plenty more where he comes from.

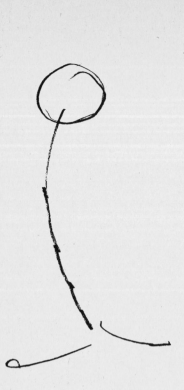

Always start with the gesture, or movement. Here's a circle and two curved lines.

Add the shapes. A rectangle for a hat, some clothes. Add a stick, too.

That stick becomes a harmonica. Add a tie and baggy pants. The rest is easy.

Except, of course, playing the harmonica. That's hard.

This little man plays the harmonica very well. Nobody stops
to listen, except the cats. They have nothing else to do.

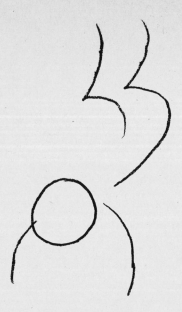

What's this going to be? We need two sideways V's, a round head, and two curved arms.

Here's a skin diver, as soon as you draw fins, fat nose, and a round mask.

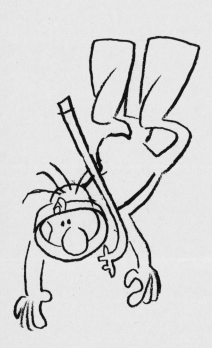

Skin diving is a lot of fun. Add a snorkel for breathing.

You get to see all sorts of things under water.

And all sorts of things get to see you.

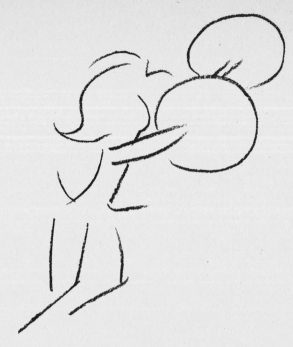

Give us three circles and two lines!

Give us some bouncy hair and lines for legs!

She has pep! She has spirit! She has eyes and a smiling mouth!

She's a high school pom-pom girl!

Unfortunately, <u>this</u> high school is very small and only has a chess team. Rah! Rah! Rah!

Let's do a teacher. A round head and some curves. She's a special kind of teacher.

Her hat is shaped like your thumb. Give her curved arms and long, curved lines for body and legs.

She's a dancing teacher. She has a ponytail.

Fill in legs and body. What kind of dancing teacher is she?

She dances in the chorus.

Let's draw a graceful person. She starts with a circle and four lines.

She's a ballerina. Her legs are curved lines. One leg is up and one is down on the ground.

Ballerinas have long, graceful gestures. Give her a tutu, long fingers, and a curved hairdo.

She loves to dance.

She dances in the chorus.

Ballerinas are not the only graceful people. Start with a long curve with a bump in it. Add a circle and three more curves.

Bullfighters are graceful, too. Add a hat and feet.

He has graceful, fluid movements. Finish his sword and clothes. Start his cape.

Everybody loves to watch bullfighters . . .

. . . especially the bulls.

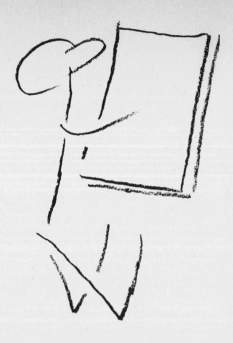

We saved the best for last. Draw a rectangle and a head that looks like a duck's head. Some straight lines, and we're off to a good start.

Draw this one with love and care. Add a chair, feet, and even hair.

Put everything you have into this one.

It's a picture of a cartoonist!

So now you can draw and color people! Right? Keep at it. Don't just copy what you see here, make up people, make up situations, have fun, and draw!